JESUS CHRIST SUPERSTAR

LYRICS by TIM RICE
MUSIC by ANDREW LLOYD WEBBER

EASY-TO-PLAY PIANO ARRANGEMENTS
by DENES AGAY

CONTENTS

ISBN 978-0-7935-2099-2

HAL•LEONARD®
CORPORATION
7777 W. BLUEMOUND RD. P.O. BOX 13819 MILWAUKEE, WI 53213

Visit Hal Leonard Online at
www.halleonard.com

SUPERSTAR

Words by TIM RICE
Music by ANDREW LLOYD WEBBER

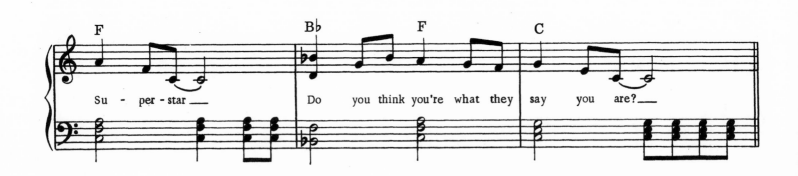

I ONLY WANT TO SAY (GETHSEMANE)

Words by TIM RICE
Music by ANDREW LLOYD WEBBER

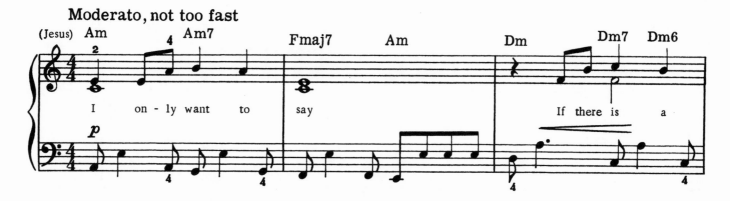

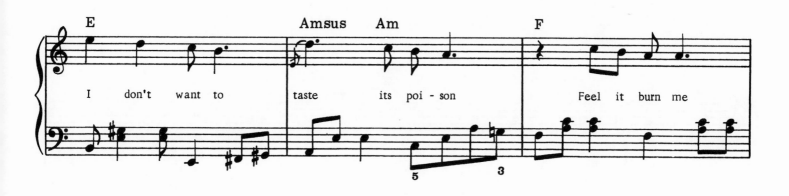

9

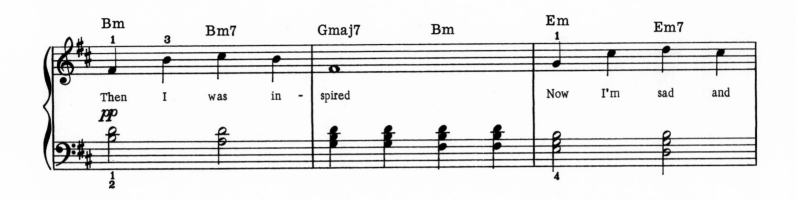

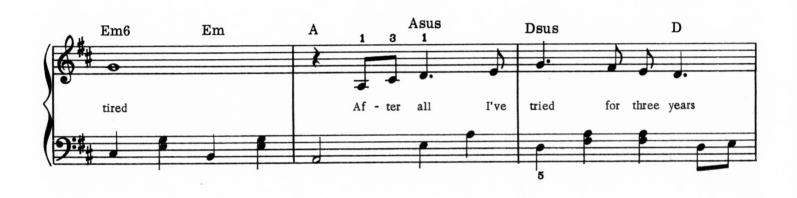

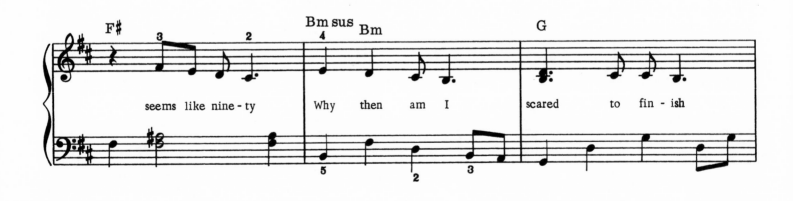

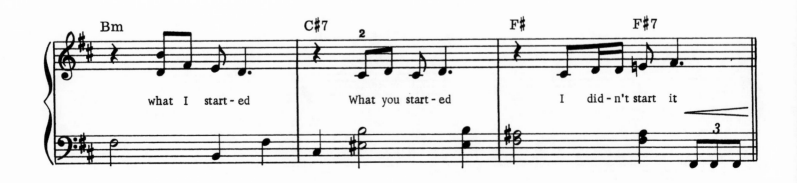

Majestically

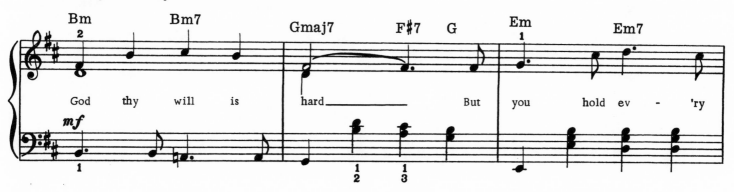

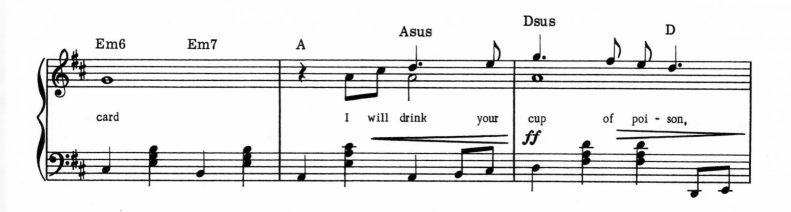

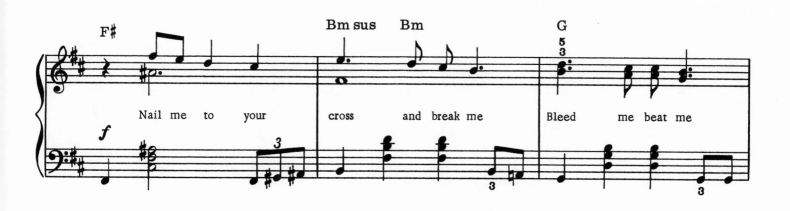

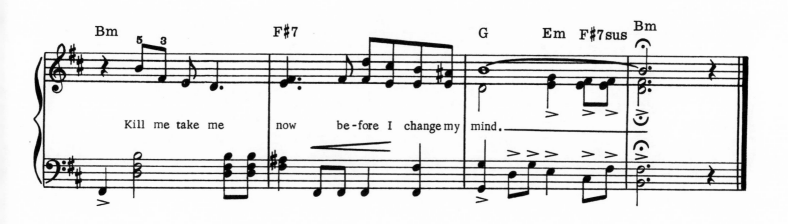

EVERYTHING'S ALRIGHT

Words by TIM RICE
Music by ANDREW LLOYD WEBBER

Smoothly

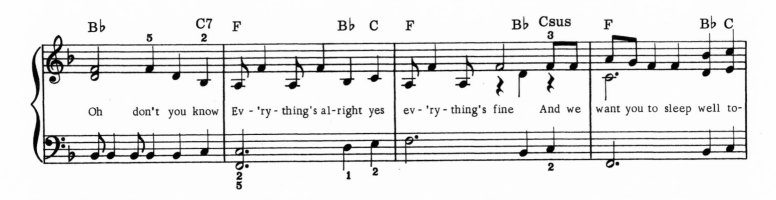

I DON'T KNOW HOW TO LOVE HIM

Words by TIM RICE
Music by ANDREW LLOYD WEBBER

Slowly, Tenderly and Very Expressively

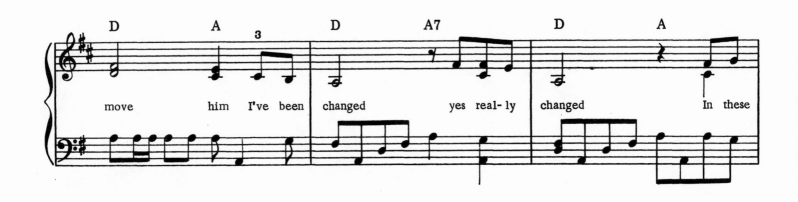

HOSANNA

Words by TIM RICE
Music by ANDREW LLOYD WEBBER

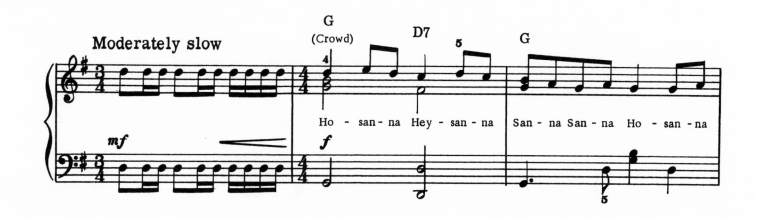

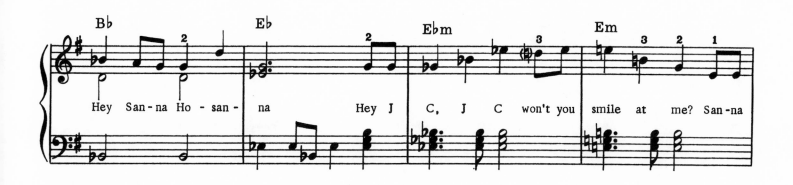

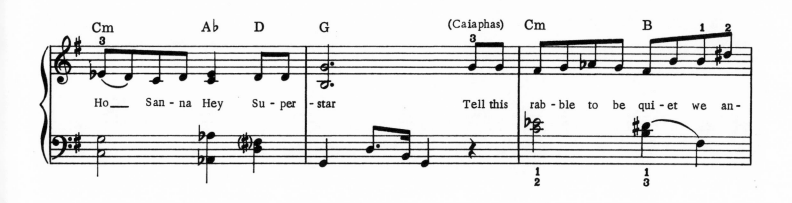

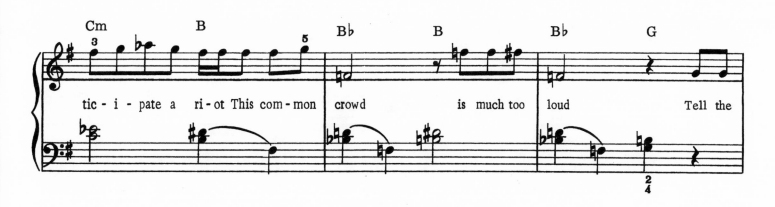

KING HEROD'S SONG

Words by TIM RICE
Music by ANDREW LLOYD WEBBER

Moderato, ad lib.

Je - sus I am o - ver - joyed to meet you face to face You've been get - ting quite a name

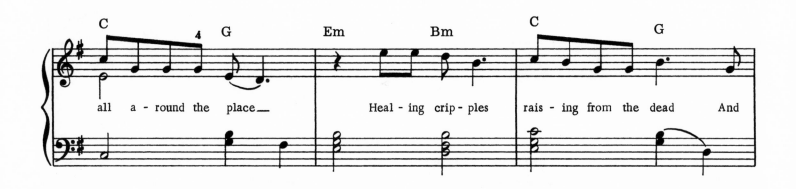

all a - round the place___ Heal - ing crip - ples rais - ing from the dead And

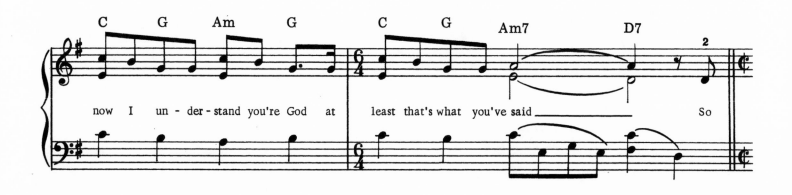

now I un - der - stand you're God at least that's what you've said___ So

Moderato, Ragtime style

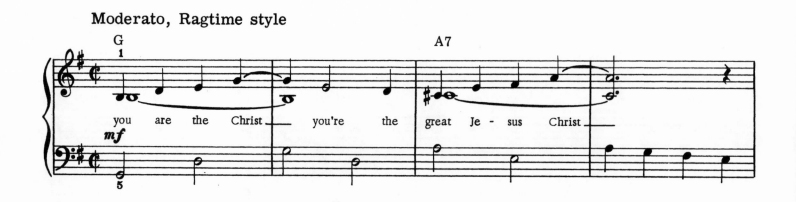

you are the Christ___ you're the great Je - sus Christ___

HEAVEN ON THEIR MINDS

Words by TIM RICE
Music by ANDREW LLOYD WEBBER

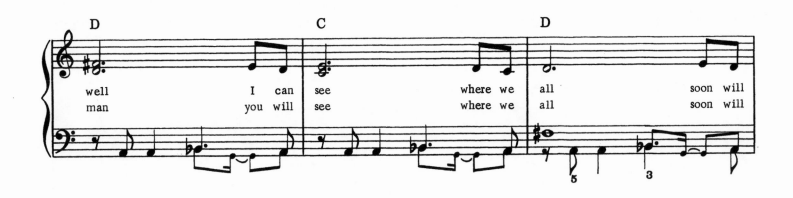

keep in our place? We are oc-cu-pied have you for-got-ten how put

down we are?_____ I am fright-ened by the crowd

For we are get-ting much too loud___ And they'll

crush us if we go too far_____ If we

go _____ too_____ far _____